# A Spiritual Awakening
## Acronyms and Poems

by

Henry Lewis and Nicholis Earnings

DORRANCE PUBLISHING CO
EST. 1920
PITTSBURGH, PENNSYLVANIA 15238

Dorrance Publishing Co
585 Alpha Drive
Suite 103
Pittsburgh PA, 15238
Visit our website at *www.dorrancebookstore.com*

ISBN: 978-1-4809-4533-3
eISBN: 978-1-4809-4510-4

# A Spiritual Awakening

# Dad

I never knew my dad very much

But in my heart I love him a whole bunch

Even though he died and passed

His memory will forever last

I love my dad with all my soul

When I rejoin him I will try to be bold

# Darkest Hour

Hearing about my dad's death was my darkest hour

But instead of my pain I make it my power

I know he is not troubled by pain or grief

With this I have my relief

We must not dread on pain of ones we lose

For this is not a choice we choose

I know I'll see my dad again

When I do he'll be my friend

Maybe then my heart will mend

We must not cry for the ones that have pass

For they have gone to meet their maker at last

# Darkest Night

Even in the darkest night

There burns a light

Although it is out of sight

To my heart it brings might

The light is truth

We never see as a youth

For as we grow old

The ones we love we hold

Even though we don't always respect

In time we reflect

So in the darkest of night

Hold on to that inner light

# Eternal grace

The eternal grace it's love will embrace

This truth will never erase

It surrounds us all

It lifts us up when we fall

It allowed me to meet my friend and brother

It even gave me an amazing mother

For the eternal grace has blessed me in such a way

For this I will never sway

Because of the eternal grace I say

Amen is the thing I pray

# Eyes

I see people's eyes

I see the secrets and lies

The eyes lead deep inside

With the emotions they hide

Eyes let people see

But never tell them what to be

Eyes are the window into the soul

As well as stories they hold.

# Family

Family is a wonderful thing

Even with all the emotions it will bring

We argue and we fight

But we always stay together thanks to God's light

Words get spoken things get said

Sometimes so bad we can't go to bed

When we grow we move away

But in our hearts the love will never sway

# Forgiveness

When we hold a grudge it makes our spirit stiff

But when we learn forgiveness our spirits lift

Our children see the emotions we send

It's shocking to see how easy minds will bend

God's word is love thy neighbor

So why can't we change our behavior

So don't bare a mind of hate

Learn forgiveness before it's too late

# Free Thy Soul

Free thy soul from the binds of hate

So thee may change before it's too late

Hate only brings fear

To his eye it brings a tear

Free thy soul you will see

His kingdom is how it should be

For His will is grace

for the human race

# Grief

Every day it gets harder and harder to find work

And it seems like around every corner crime will lurk

Every day we hide behind a mask

Is it because we are afraid of our everyday task

We seem to sometimes ignore our hearts

Because we fear that it will tear us apart

We don't realize the pain of losing the ones we hold dear

But we always wonder why we are afraid to shed a tear

We hold it in unseeing how it hurts another

Even the dead one's lover

So what is grief you ask?

To me it's always hiding beneath the mask

# Hate and Fear

The world is filled with fear

It makes me shed a tear

This fear only brings hate

We need to change before it's too late

Life can be so much more

If we love the ones we ignore

Can we rid the world of hate and fear in time?

This is the question that leaves my mind in a bind

I think we can if we work with one another

Only once we treat the world like we were brothers

We fear what we do not understand

All because our ideas we force as we demand

To rid the world of hate and fear we inflict

We must settle our difference and end the conflict.

# Hate

I'm so sick and tired of hearing

someone say they hate another

When we should be trying

to love each other like brothers

When we hate life passes us by

Before you know it you die

So don't go and say you hate all around

Don't you know you're setting yourself

to go into the ground

So don't go around hating

Man don't you see your life is wasting.

# Heavenly Earth

The earth is full of beautiful things

Peace to me is what it brings

I see now the way things are

My heart no longer has bars

Heavenly earth is my song

With friends and family is where I belong

I hope one day the world will know

Like plants we need to grow

This heavenly earth is not a defection

But the soul of our reflection

As time marches on

The anger I feel is gone

For this heavenly earth has healed me

Just the way God intended it to be

This heavenly earth is not a toy

It is meant for us all to enjoy.

# Life

We go around not seeing life's bad

as if we couldn't see

Even when we got people in the military

being all they can be

What I don't get is people waste their life

Arguing with their wife

We go around as if we are blind

All because we refuse to open our mind

We go around in strife

All because we don't love what we got in life.

# Look Inside

Look inside your heart

Does the image tear you apart

Do you like what you see

Is it who you really want to be

Do you want to be something more

Like those songs in stories of lore

Look inside one more time

Isn't it funny how things change on a dime.

# Look into My Mind

Look into my mind

I don't know what you will find

With all the thoughts I see

They sometimes tend to scare me

They do know strike fear

Sometimes they make you shed a tear

You can look into my mind if you can

But most of the time it is a place I ban

People judge me for what I say

But just look into my mind for a day.

# Love and Courage

Love and courage is something we need

It is as important as the air we breathe

Love and courage is within our hearts

It is the thing that keeps us from being torn apart

For when we have both we are strong

It is with this strength we know we belong

If we could all just learn to get along

Then we could all sing the same song

# Loved Ones

I spend time with the ones I love

Because they make my heart fly higher than a dove

I love my niece and nephew with all my heart

No matter what nothing can tear that apart

I'd give my life for them without a thought

Because into this world

those children my sister brought

# Mothers

We love our mother yes we do

Even though some may find it hard to be true

We get on their nerves quite a bit

As children we often throw a fit

Mothers cook and work or clean all day long

They even teach us right from wrong

Without them we wouldn't sing

Because into this world the children they bring

Mothers love their children no matter what

Even when they act like a butt

# My Life

I'm thankful for the things in my life

I'm even thankful for the strife

Because of it I know who I want to be

And that person is me

I learn new things every day

I learn them in my own way

I wouldn't change one thing about me

All the pain and joy made me who I want to be

So what's the best thing in my life you say

It's the people and things that light the way

# My Life

Every day I hang out with my friend

With his words my mind does mend

He teaches me so much

What he says my heart it does touch

My life is stressed

Yet my life is so blessed

I have learned so much in my life

Even though yet I don't have a wife.

# Paving

I'm paving the way to happiness

with these two hands of mine

When I know its hard cause there is no line

We go around in the dark searching for the light

Even though sometimes it's so bright

This puts us in so much hurt

So we go around making others feel as low as dirt

So can't you see me waving

I'm so hoping you'll start paving.

# Peace of mind

I know this is new

Well the feelings are true.

I do not know me and I do not know you

I do know I walk around in a bind

I do this all the time

Searching around for something to find

To give me some peace of mind

The smoke I see blinds my eye

I know the day will come when I will die

There is a fine line between life and death

So enjoy every breath

I love everything that is mine

I realize my family gives me piece of mind.

# Poem I Food for Thought

So hey count to two,

I will do and be true,

Through and through like mike

Climbing the pike,

Oh no yikes,

Will you like,

My book of sikes.

# Poem II Nine Fruits of the Spirit

Lovingly, joyously, peacefully,

Patiently, kindly, goodly,

Faithfully, gently, self-controlled,

Alive give me five,

I am king bee in a honey hive,

So let me do a little jive!

# Poem III Brainstorm

Vocabulary on the contrary,

Becomingly, thoughtfully, carefully,

Designingly, understandably going to stand

Here beside Mr. Lee.

# Poem IV Life

Let individuals forgive each other

cause who am I to say what's what,

I am just Mr. Smiley and I know

I can smite thee and watch thee

Stumble as I

Remain humble,

Oh no you might crumble under the improbable,

Is it undeniable that I am the irresistible,

And I am the inevitable

But not entirely impossible

# Poem V Light Dark

Live in glorified holiness truthfully,

Destined angel is knowledgably,

Wisely, understandingly, listening

To every word said by thee

So let's all go to the heavenly keeper of light

And leave the dark behind

And allow the blind to see all that can be

# Poem VI Live

Love is very exceptional,

So please don't obliterate obstante,

In the rates and please don't put me in a crate,

Cause I will incinerate the cage,

These walls look beige,

Why can't they just give me a ball to play with,

Oh well I won't dwell long in the belly of this whale,

One day he will open up his mouth

and let me be free,

Just so I can see,

oh what my pretty eyes will do to thee,

A wise man once said to me, "what will be will be"

# Poem VII Life

Live in freedom eternally

But work hard for a living accordingly,

Construction for a consequently better life,

Moral is set small goals

then work your way to the bigger ones,

Then consequently the endingly accomplishments

will show that

You can do and be true

so please be a doer not a talker but a listener,

It takes great courage to do the walk so take some chalk,

Do a little hop scotch with your kids

Cause we only get one life like one world one love

So treat it as if it were your last

and take care of this world and the one love

If together we can make an effort cause it takes teamwork

# Poem VIII World

## <u>W</u>ill <u>O</u>f <u>R</u>eal <u>L</u>ife <u>D</u>iadem

Can you see it's not seeing that is believing,

It is faith and self-control that I found the lords crown,

And I didn't clown around in returning it to him,

Just like a wise man once said to me

you got to pull it around to the front,

Almost as if I were the captain of this boat,

Kind of like swimming you have to learn how to float,

Just like learning how to be a great leader

you must first follow

That's why my fellow neighbor taught me a little poetry

So one day I could tell my story

this is for my best friend and brother Henry!

# Poem IX

The rising under the healing will be true,

So please don't feel blue,

Cause I will do,

Only if you say I love you,

All in all we will be true,

For the few it will be hard to do,

If you know this to be true then say I do,

Cause it is overdue!

# Poem X Peace

Please eternal angel carry everyone

so that one day I can say I have won the Nobel

Peace prize until then I cannot say that I am done,

Or maybe I will stay in my own little world

and call myself number one

Even though I am number eight so let's get it straight,

Then I might be alright so hang on tight

because I might give you a fright,

But I will still call knowledge power

and it will be my mighty weapon,

So watch out I will control a whole legion

maybe even the nations,

So all aboard this train and don't be absurd

it took a great deal of patience

To get this good and now I am out of the mood

So now this poem has been gone and done,

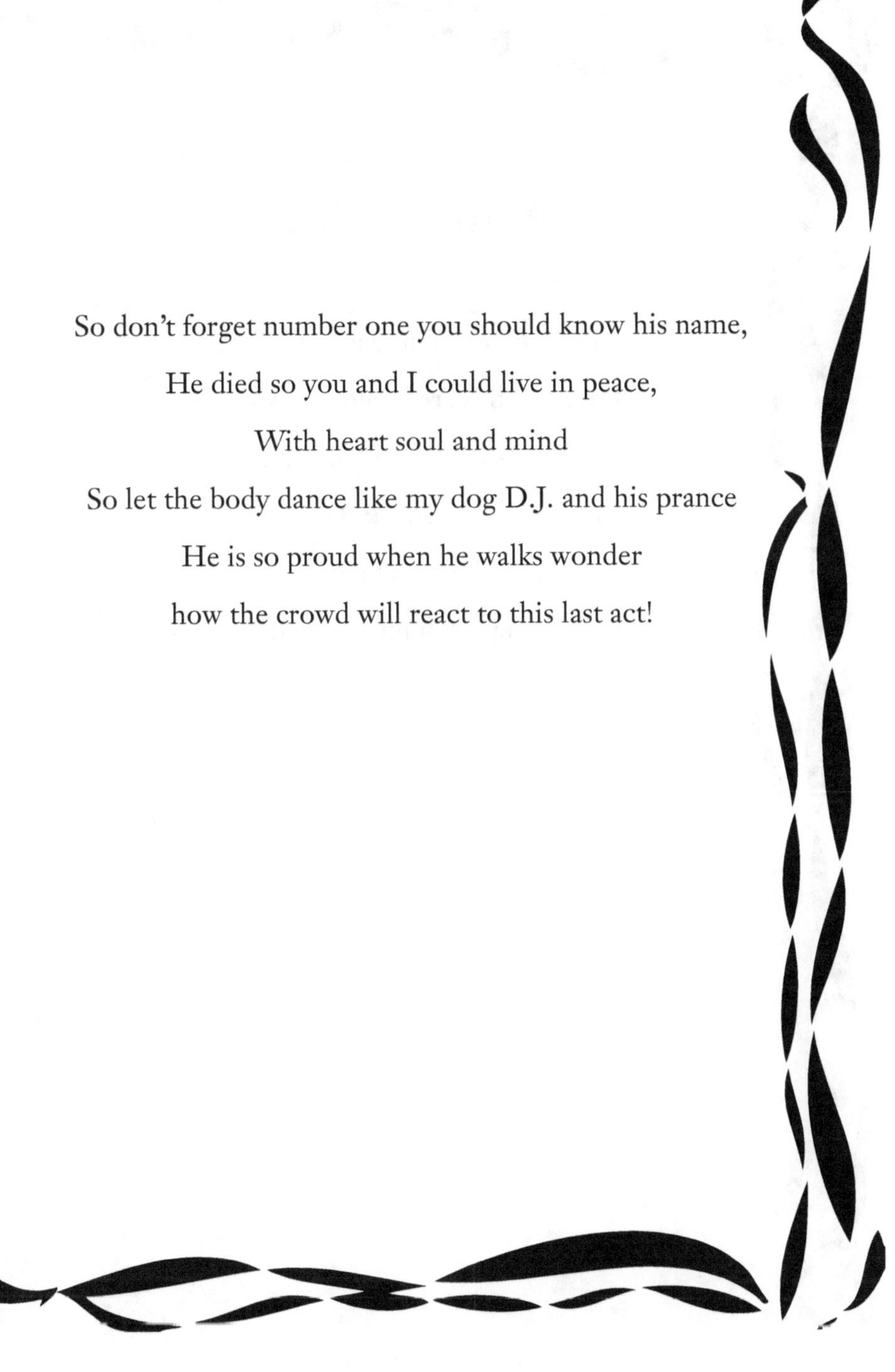

So don't forget number one you should know his name,

He died so you and I could live in peace,

With heart soul and mind

So let the body dance like my dog D.J. and his prance

He is so proud when he walks wonder

how the crowd will react to this last act!

# Poem II Paul

Peaceful angel understands life,

So I must be careful along my strife,

Andy Griffith and Barney Fife

was a great moralistic show to watch

So I will try to be realistic

and stay fantastic in my one and only life

# Poem XII Time

As I look at the clock it says time to take the dogs for a walk

As I sit here and think of a rhyme it goes tick tock,

I might have to call the doc,

But he will just give me some crock,

So I think I will just knock for the time

to make a rhyme

Oh no do you have the time cause I am in my prime,

Maybe for a small portion of your time

I will rhyme for a dime

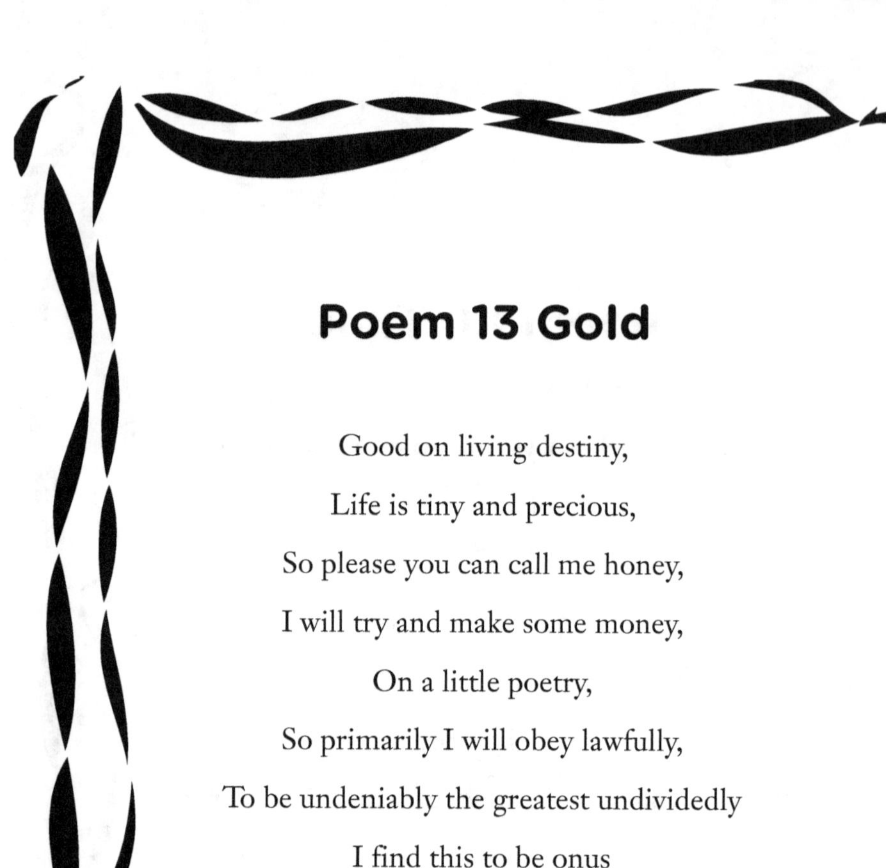

# Poem 13 Gold

Good on living destiny,

Life is tiny and precious,

So please you can call me honey,

I will try and make some money,

On a little poetry,

So primarily I will obey lawfully,

To be undeniably the greatest undividedly

I find this to be onus

# Poem XIV Silver

Savior initializes life's various exceptional realities,

So please do count the qualities

because it is not about the quantities,

It is about all the exceptionalities and personalities,

I am the beginning and end of destinies,

So please give a hug and kiss to your enemies

# Poem XV Jesus
# and the Cross

He came and took the blame,

Wonder if he ever played a game,

Did he know his name would go down in fame?

I am glad he came to take the blame,

I would love to play a game with him,

When he comes to claim his fame,

Did you know his cross

was his sword bright with flame

For me cross stands for

continuously righteously organizingly saving sinners!

# Poem XVII Holy

<u>H</u>ope <u>O</u>ver <u>L</u>iving <u>Y</u>outh,

Giving over receiving love

Smoothly allowing over defending booth,

Beginning over an ending truth

# Poem XVII
# Rolling the Stone

Could you be so kind to throw me a bone,

Jesus was buried behind the stone,

He rolled it away and took a seat on the throne,

Wonder if he planned his way home,

Kind of like "E.T. phone home."

# Poem IXX Blind

So can I help the blind in such a way they will find

The most structurally blinded hiding behind the stone,

Then they can grind as they are blind,

Then as the stone dissipates the bound will be free

The light will allow your heart to see

Oh wouldn't that be kind,

A way to free Jesus to his rightful throne,

Then we will all be on our way home,

Through the lights embrace and his eternal love

# Poem XXI Dove

Oh please find the dove,

With the ecstatic love,

I will heave and hove

To try and move that stone,

On my own then I will hover over the clouds,

Man my grandpa would be proud

I wonder if my father would be proud

Would he let me sit on his throne

Then I could say I am king of this world

If only I memorize the word

# Tears of joy

I will try,

If I cry,

Please do not pry,

I will give the gift of rye!

# Poetry

I dream of a life of something more

Because sitting around is such a bore

I see a lot of things that make me upset

So I write poetry just for an outlet

So when you're upset write poetry down

And you'll find your heart will be unbound.

# Point of view

I was born an angry person

But that's only one version

I hide out in my comfort zone

In my room I stay alone

I look at both points of view

I see the old as well as the new

It is so easy to sway from the light

It is not so simple as day or night.

# See

You see that it is life

You see that man with his wife

He's living his life

You see this happiness is bliss

You see him or is the image to dim

You know what I see?

I see a man who couldn't see

What life could be.

# Spoken

If you read my poems you know the words I have spoken

Now here's my appreciation just a small token

But here's what you didn't know

My mind works quiet slow

But that doesn't mean my words

won't make you get up and go

I'm not a person of wealth

But I do have my health

I may not be the most important person

But I am a person of my own version

I am not a being of high class

But the words I say cut like glass

# The Dark

I feel myself slipping into the dark

While next door the dogs bark

I no longer see the line

Maybe it's time for my mind to redefine

Am I nothing but a shell?

As I hear the ringing of a bell

My mind has gone black

Is it something I lack?

But I won't let myself slip away

I am me and I'm here to stay

# The Light

Most people walk around not seeing the light

Even when it is so bright

They close their eyes and head to strife

They turn their backs on life

This is not the way to be

The light sets us free

The dark only makes us bend

Embrace the light and you will mend

So what is the light you ask?

The answer is no simple task

For me the light is God

For some it might seem odd

But it is the truth without and end

All I can say is amen.

# The Soul

The soul is a story untold

But when we meet our maker the story unfolds

We never see this thing

But we hear the thoughts it does bring

So what is the soul

What secrets does it really hold

When we die we rejoin the spirits of old.

# The World

I see the goodness in the world

All as time makes it twirl

I see the light as it touches the ground

Even to the smallest ant mound

The world is a beautiful place

And we are all just one big race

Under God's eternal grace

# Until Then

God judges us when we die

He holds us accountable for every lie

We live in fear of that day

So much we ignore the words

our mind tell us to say

I don't live in fear of how and when

I'll live my life from now until then

# Wondering

I find myself wondering from time to time

Just a little thing of mine

I dislike the things I see

What happened to the way things used to be

I start wondering why my friends move away

Leaving me here in this place I stay

My heart feels like it has bars

As my feet are scorched by the hot tar

I am always wondering about my dad

When I heard he died it made me sad

The pain I felt was nothing new

Compared to the pain of the ones he knew.

Now, most of these poems are done by my friend. The numbered ones are the ones I tried. We inspired each other. I helped him with his poems, and he helped me with the next part of this book, which is made up of four hundred acronyms. I ended up doing in one month, and believe me, it was nerve wracking. I guess I deserved it since I did the same thing to my friend. We were having a deep conversation and I ended up making him come up with fifteen poems in less than five minutes, just by the few words. I said don't remember what was said either in the month. I decided to do the acronyms I did one for each book of the *Gideon's Bible*. I had a wild spiritual experience when I was twenty that told me I was Jesus reincarnated but I am twenty-seven now and I learned recently I just want to be me and that's a wild child who believes in God, but remembers that I make my religion up as I go so like my grandfather told me I may never be right but I am never wrong so therefore I will sing my song. Part of the experience I ended up reading revelations and learned that my grandparents and their five kids were the seven holy spirits and that I was number eight. Also I have a hurricane on the left side of my face when I have a five o'clock shadow; it looks like a spiral and the eternal life symbol is like that on the pyramids. I also have a huge dimple in my chin that people have told me is a touch from God. I have been on medications for my belief since I was twenty. I have had problems with my mind racing and suicidal thoughts. I have never acted on it except once when I was fifteen and got alcohol poisoning.

Both my friend and I have had mental issues. We both are on disability for it. We both have had our ups and downs but most importantly we remember to enjoy the moment and laugh more than anything. I taught him how to cook eggs and fried chicken. It's not about the obstacles in life, its' about the journey and what you do with the time that is given to you—don't waste it. I am trying to help both of us by having this book published. He and I are stuck at home with our parents and we just want to travel and eat at different places because we love food. We call ourselves heaven and nature because of my blue eyes and his green eyes. Also, I am the one with white horse. He was born during the year of the horse and I was born during the year of the snake. I call him my staff and my other neighbor is the rod. The seven and the three of us are getting older. My biggest fear is living in this life without them. I love almost all of my friends—they are like family. Not only am I born during the year of the snake, but I am also a Virgo. It's Sep. 16, 2017. A person once told me I am a tool of God but if I try to be good at it, it doesn't work, but if I just be myself then I am good at it. I can't tell you how many bad things I have been through because I don't keep track. I keep track of my victories and celebrations/feasts.


**AAA:** all angels arise

**ACRONYMS:** angel crowned rules over nations youthfully mending souls

**ACROSS:** angels continuously righteously organizationally saving souls

**ACRUX:** Angels' captain really understands xebec

**ACTION:** angels calling true intellectuals of nations

**ACTS:** Angels continue to save

**AGLET:** angel greatly loves eternal truth

**AGLET:** angels' gifts let everyone trust

**AMEN:** angels motivate everyone now

**AMEN:** angels move everywhere now

**AMEN:** angels move eternally now

**AMOS:** angel master of saved

**ANGELS:** all nations gather everywhere living soulfully

**ARK:** angel really knows

**ARK:** angels rescue knowledge

**ARK:** angels' righteous knowledge

**ARK:** angels' random knowledge

**ARK:** angels rain knowledge

**ARMS:** Austin rescues man's salvation

**ARMS:** angels rescue men slowly

**ARMS;** angel's righteous men saving

**ARMS:** angels raise men specifically

**ASTROLOGY:** angels save the righteous over love of god's youthfulness

**AUSSIE:** angel understands saving souls is eternal

**AUSTIN:** angels understand sustaining truth in nations

**AUSTIN:** Angel's universal savior talks infinitely now

**APPLE:** all people's personalities live emotionally

**A.L.S:** angel loves saving

**ALS:** angel lives strong


**BABTIST:** believers arise before the intellectual saving truth

**BABYLON:** be all believingly youthfully lovingly over nation-alities

**BEAUTY:** beautiful eternal angel understands the youth

**BIBLE:** believing individuals being loved eternally

**BLIND:** believers live infinitely now determined

**BLUE:** blessed lives understandably eternally

**BLUE:** bless lives understandingly everywhere

**BLUE:** bless life understanding eternity

**BOO:** blessed of overall

**BOX:** bring on xebec

**BOX:** believers on xebec

**BOX;** brighten over xebec

**BRAINS:** bestowing righteous angels in neutral salvation

**BOY:** basic overall youth

**BULL:** beautiful understanding loving lives

**BULL:** beautiful understanding living love

**BUS:** believers understand savior


**CAPTIVATED:** crowned angel protects the individuals' various actions to eternal days

**CHAIN:** cases have angel initializing now

**CHAIN:** Christ has angels in nations

**CHERRY:** cause healing everywhere righteously reassuring youth

**CHRONICLES:** calling heavens realities over new initial classes, lecturing evolving sinner

**CITY HAVE ENTRANCE:** careful instructors tell youth how angels' vision eventually enters new traditions rallying all now constantly everywhere

**CLEAN;** Christ loves everywhere always now **HOUSE;** having overall understanding settle everyone

**CLEAR;** Christ's love equals all religions

**CLEAR;** Christ's love equals all realities

**CLEAR;** Christ's love equals all rise

**CLEAR;** cross lures eternal angel's righteousness

**CLOCK;** Christ lives over careful knowledge

**COLLAGE;** call of living lovers always gentle everywhere

**COLLEGE;** call of legion leaders equally growing everywhere

**COLOSSIANS;** call over life on saint's strength initializing angels new savior

**CONCOURSE;** call of now coming over understanding realities saving everyone

**CORINTHIANS;** can overall reality initialize nevertheless true haven in angels new salvation

**CROSS;** constellations rise over sustaining spirits

**CROSS;** conscious realities of sustaining souls

**CROSS;** Christ's righteous offering saves souls

**CROSS;** conscious realities over soothing streams

**CROSS;** continuously righteously organizingly saving souls


**DAD;** decisions always dedicated

**DANIEL;** divine angel now initializes eternal life

**DARK;** deciding angels' random knowledge

**DEAD;** dedicated eternal angels decisions

**DESTINY;** destiny entrusts savior to initializing new youthfulness

**DEUTERONOMY;** dexterity even uses the evergreens retribution over new onus multiplying youthfulness

**DEVIL;** divine eternal vision initiates life

**DIAMOND;** divine infinite angels multiplies ongoing new destinies/decisions

**DOGGY;** divinity over god's greatest youth


**EARTH;** even/eternal angels rescue the humans

**EARTH;** xebec angels reassure the heard

**EARTH;** xebec arrives righteously to heaven

**EARTH;** every angel raises truth here

**EARTH;** every angled reality turn here

**EARTH;** eternal angels' real truth here

**EARTH;** eternal angel raise the heaven

**EARTH;** even angels respect the humans

**EARTH;** even angels rise to humans

**EARTH;** eventually all realize true heaven

**ECCLESIASTES;** emotions can cause loving evergreens soil's inner self allowing sustainment to eternal savior

**EFFECT;** eternal falling forefathers enlighten conscious truth

**EIGHT;** enlightened insightful, gifted healing truth/trinity

**ELEVATE;** eternal life eventually values all truth equally

**EMBRACE;** eternal men's bravery reassures artillery constantly everywhere

**EMBRACE;** every man believes righteous angel's conscious eternally

**EMBRACE;** eternal men's bravery reassure all constantly everywhere

**EMOTIONS;** eternal mothers of the individuals over new souls

**ENIGMA;** eternal new intellectual god masters all

**ENTER;** eternal new truth everywhere righteously

**EPHESIANS;** eternal prophet hears every sinner, initial angel now stronger

**ESTHER;** evergreen sustains the healing everywhere righteously

**EXODUS;** eternal xebec over destinies under sail

**EZEKIEL;** Eternal Zeus's evergreens kindness initializes eternal life

**EZRA;** eternal Zeus raises angels


**FAITH;** father angel is the healer

**FAITHFUL;** fallen angel is the heavens fulfillment under love

**FAMILY;** father angel mends intellectually living youth

**FATHER;** father angels truth heals everyone's reality

**FIRE;** free individuals righteously eternally

**FIVE;** father is very excepting

**FIVE;** father intellectually envisioning everyone

**FIVE;** followers intellectually visionary excepts

**FIVE;** followers individually view everything

**FLY;** father loving youth

**FOUR;** father over understanding realities

**FOUR;** fathers of understanding realities

**FREE;** father's real eternal evergreen

**FRUITS;** freedom redeeming unites individual true spirits


**GALATIANS;** god's angels love Austin to initialize always now saving

**GATE;** gathering angels to earth

**GATHERING;** God's angels' truth healing everyone righteously individually now growing

**GENESIS;** God eternally never exits sends initialed son

**GENESIS;** God's evergreen now eternal, so is savior

**GENTLE;** give eternally now, the love everywhere

**GIDEONS;** god is dividing everyone on new subtleties

**GIDEONS;** god is deciding everyone's ongoing new substantionalities

**GIDEONS;** good individuals deciding every ongoing new soul

**GIRL;** God is really living

**GIRL;** God is really loving

**GLORY;** God's love over real youth

**GLORY HILL;** God's love over real youth having individual living lovers

**GOD;** good on destinies

**GOLD;** God over loving destinies

**GOLD;** God of loving destinations

**GOLD;** God of living diadem

**GOLD;** Good old leader does

**DIGGER;** does instrumentally gliding graciously everywhere righteously

**GOOD;** God of overall destinies

**GRACE;** God raises angels continuously everywhere

**GRACE;** God's real angels calling everyone

**GRAPE;** God raises all personalities emotionally

**GREAT;** God's righteous eternal angels' team

**GREEN;** God's realities evenly everywhere now

**GREEN;** God's righteous earth eternal now

**GREEN;** God rests eventually everywhere now


**HABAKKUK;** having angel being all kind knowing understanding knowledge

**HAGGAI;** have angels gathering goods always intellectually

**HAND;** hoping allow new destinies

**HAND;** healing all new destinies

**HAPPY;** heaven's angel people pleasing youth

**HAT;** hear angel's truth

**HATE;** healing all the exceptionalities

**HATE;** have angels talk equally

**HEAL;** have eternal angels love

**HEAL;** hopefully eternal angel lives

**HEAL;** healing everyone allowing life

**HEART;** healing eternal angels' real truth

**HEART;** heavenly eternal angel raises truth

**HEAVEN;** healing eternal angels' vengeance everywhere now

**HEAVEN;** healing eternal angel very exceptional now

**HEAVEN;** healing every angels' vision everywhere now

**HEBREWS;** having eternal belief realizing everyone's with savor

**HELL;** heaven eternally loves life

**HELL;** healing every living life

**HELL;** healing every loving life

**HIGH;** healing individuals gently here

**HILL;** heaven initials living lives

**HILL;** healing individual living lovers

**HOLD;** healing of living dead

**HOLD;** healing over life decisions

**HOLD;** heaven over living diadem

**HOLY;** hope over living youth

**HOLY;** heaven over living youth

**HOLY;** healing over living youth

**HOME;** healing/ hope over men everywhere/eternally

**HOPE;** healing over people everywhere

**HOPE;** heaven of personal entities

**HOPE;** heaven overcomes peace eternally

**HOSEA;** heaven over saving eternal angel

**HOSEA;** heaven of saving eternal angel

**HOSEA;** healing on saving everyone always

**HOUR;** heaven over understanding realities

**HUMANS;** healing understanding men always now saved


**IMPOSSIBLE;** intellectually mending population of sustaining souls is basic loving earth

**IN;** individual newbies

**INSPIRATIONS;** insightful new spirit prophesying in rational allegations to initialize on nations salvation

**INTELLECTUALS;** inspiring nations to eternal loving life eventually causes true understanding angels love spirituality

**ISAIAH;** individual saving angel is all hearing


**JAKIAH;** Jesus' angels' kindness is all hearing

**JAKIAH;** Jewish angels' kindness is all heavens

**JAMES;** Jesus' angels meet every Sabbath

**JAMES;** just angels meet every Sabbath

**JEREMIAH;** Jesus enlightens redeemed entering master's initialized angels' heaven

**JEWELS;** Jesus eventually wins every loving soul

**JOEL;** Jesus over eternal life

**JOB;** Jesus over believers

**JOHN;** Jesus over heaven now

**JONAH;** Jesus over nations' angels' heavens

**JOSHUA;** just over sweet heaven under angels

**JOSHUA;** Jesus of sweet heaven under angels

**JOY;** Jesus over youth

**JOY;** Jews of Yahweh

**JUDE;** Jesus under destinies everywhere


**KINGDOMS;** knowledge is now growing down over men slowly

**KINGDOMS;** kindness infinitely now grows down over men slowly

**KIND;** knowledge is now divine

**KINDNESS;** knowledgeable intellectuals now decide new

eternal soul sustainment

**KING;** knowledge is now growing

**KING;** kindness is now growing

**KING;** knowledge is now god's

**KINGS;** kindness is now god's saints

**KNOTS;** kindly newly omniscient truth spiritually

**KNOTS;** kindly newly omnisciently true spirituality

**KNOW;** knowledge now over world

**KNOW;** kindness now over world


**LAKE;** love angels knowledge eternally

**LAMENTATIONS;** let all master's eternal nationalities take all the initializing over new schools/Sabbath

**LAMENTATIONS;** let all men everywhere now take all the inscriptions over new schools/Sabbath

Lamentations stands for god having no limitations

**LAW;** live all wisely

**LAW;** life always wins

**LEE;** live eternal evergreen

**LIFE;** live intellectually for eternity

**LIFE;** live in freedom eternally

**LIFE;** let individuals farm eternally

**LIFE;** love individuals for eternity

**LIGHTNING;** let individuals get healing to new insights now growing

**LIGHT;** let individuals get healing truth

**LIGHT;** live in gentle heaven together

**LOVE;** live on various expectations

**LOVE;** love over various emotions

**LOVE;** living of various exceptionalities

**LIVE;** let individuals view equality

**LIVE;** love individual various exceptionalities

**LIVE;** let individuals view everyone

**LIVE;** let individuals view exceptionalities

**LOVE;** let others view emotions

**LUCK;** live under careful knowledge

**LUKE;** love understanding knowledge eternally


**MAGIC;** mending all God's individual consciousnesses

**MAIL;** mend all individual lives

**MALACH;** mankind's angels love all choices healing

**MAN;** mend all now

**MARK;** master angel really knows

**MARK;** master angel's righteous knowledge

**MASTER;** mend all souls to eternal realities

**MEN;** move eternally now

**MICAH;** man is calling angels here

**MOTHER;** mending of the humans eternally righteously

**MOM;** mending over men

**MOUTIAN;** men of understanding truth in arising nations


**NAHUM;** newest angels heaven understands master

**NAHUM;** now all heaven understands men

**NATION;** new angels truth is overhauling now

**NECK;** new eternal constant knowledge

**NEHEMIAH;** now entrusting heaven's eternal master initial-
izing angels here

**NINE;** new insight now everywhere

**NOTE;** new overall truth everywhere

**NUMBERS;** now understanding master's book eternally remembering son/sons/saviors


**OAKHILL;** over angel's knowledge having individual living lovers

**OBADIAH;** over booking/bibles angels deciding individuals always here

**OFFERING;** overhauling falling fathers enticingly reassuring intellectuals now gently

**ONE;** onus now entering

**ONE:** onus now exiting

**ONE;** overall new everyone

**ONE;** overall now everywhere

**ORANGE;** ongoing rising angels now grow everywhere

**OUTLAW;** over understanding the loving angels' wisdom

**OVER;** of visionary eternal righteousness


**PANDA;** peaceful angel now decides all

**PANDA;** please angel new decisions always

**PARKS;** peaceful angel raises knowledge slowly

**PASSION;** personal angel saves souls in overruling nations

**PASSION;** papa angel saving soulful individuals of nations

**PAUL;** peaceful angel understands life

**PEACE;** preaching equations always causing equality

**PEACE;** preaching everywhere always causing eternity

**PEACE;** please eternal angel carry everyone

**PEACE;** peaceful eternal angel raise life

**PEACEFUL;** peaceful eternal angel carries every fulfilling understanding life

**PEACEFUL;** please eternal angel carry everyone falling under love

**PEAR;** peaceful eternal angel rise

**PEARL;** please eternal angel carry everyone

**PEOPLE;** peace eternally over people loving each other

**PERCEPTION;** personal evergreen really calms everyone's personality to invite over nations

**PETER;** peace eternally to everyone's reality

**PHILEMON;** people healing individuals letting every man over nationalities

**PHILIPPIANS;** people having individual living intellectuals playing paradoxical in all new salvation

**PLANET;** prophet loves angel's new everlasting truth

**PLENTY;** please love everyone now thank you

**POEM;** peace over everyone's misfortunes

**POPULATION;** personalities of people understand loving angels truth initializing over nations

**POWER;** peace over world eventually realistic

**POWER;** pause over wisdoms eternal righteousness

**POWERS;** pause over wise eternal righteous savior

**PRIME;** prophet really is master eternally

**PRIME;** prophets reality individually mends everyone

**PRIME;** personal realms initialize man's equality

**PROVERBS;** pathways relied over visions, each real believer saved

**PS;** peace saving

**PSALM;** peaceful saving angel love man

**PSALMS;** peaceful saving angel loves man's salvation


**QUETIONS;** quests understanding eternal truth is of nations' salvation

**RAIN;** rise angels intellectually now

**RAIN;** raise angels individually now

**READY;** righteous eternal angel dances youthfully

**REALM;** righteous eternal angels love men

**REALM;** read every angels loving meaning

**RED;** righteous eternal devotion

**RED;** righteous eternal decisions

**RELY;** rise eternal living youth/yeshiva

**REVELATION;** reveling every various eternal love at the inevitable on nations

**RIGHT;** real individuals give healing truth

**ROCK;** rely on Christ's knowledge

**ROCK;** rely on continuous knowledge

**ROCK;** rely on constant knowledge

**ROLL;** rise over loving lives

**ROMANS;** reality over men's angels' new salvation

**ROMANS;** righteous of men, angels now stand

**RUTH;** righteous understanding the heavens

**RUTH;** realities understand truth here


**SAIL;** save angels initializing love

**SAMUEL;** saving angel master understands eternal life

**SAVING;** serene angels' vision is now growing

**SEAT;** saving eternal angels' truth

**SENCES;** saving everyone now causing eternal salvation

**SENCES;** saving everyone's new continuous/conscious eternal souls

**SELFCONTROL;** spirit eternally loves fulfilling contributions over new thoughts relying on life

**SEVENS;** saving earthly vessel entering new space

**SHIT;** seeing heaven is true/truth

**SIN;** saving initialized now

**SIN;** save individuals now

**SIX;** sailing inside xebec

**SILVER;** saving individuals living vary eternally righteously

**SIMPLE;** saints inspire multiple people living everywhere

**SIMPLE;** saving individuals mentally purposefully lovingly eternally

**SMITHEY;** saving men individually to having eternal youthfulness

**SOLOMON;** savior overruling life of misfortunes over nationalities

**SPIRIT;** saving people individually really improves trust

**SPIRIT;** saving prophets inspirations reeled into truthfulness

**SPIRITUAL;** saving people intellectually righteously individually that understand all life

**SPIRITUAL;** savior predicts individuals realities to understanding all life

**STAND;** savior tells angels new deliverance

**STAR;** save the angels reality

**SUN;** saving United Nations


**TEAM;** the eternal angelic men

**TEAM;** tell every angel master

**TEAM;** truth everywhere always mending

**TEAM;** truth every angel mentions

**TEAM;** true every angel mends

**TEAM;** the eternal angel's mission

**TEN;** truth everywhere now

**THE;** true holy eternity

**THE;** truth here earthlings

**THE;** true healing everywhere

**THEIR;** truth healing everyone's individual reality

**THERE;** truth having everyone's righteous eternity

**THERE;** truth healing everyone's reality everywhere

**THESSALONIANS;** true heaven's evergreen stays strong allowing love over new individual angels' new salvation

**THEY;** true holy eternal youth

**THEY;** truth healing everyone's youthfulness

**THUNDER;** truth healing under newbies deciding entering reality

**THING;** truth healing individuals now good

**THREE;** truth healing realities everywhere eternally

**THREE;** the holy righteousness eternally existing

**THY;** the holy youth

**THY;** truth heals youth

**TIME;** time individually mends everyone

**TIME;** the infinite mother earth

**TIME;** truth individually mends everyone

**TIMOTHY;** the infinite master over the holy youth/Youngman

**TITUS;** the individual truth understands sinners

**TOMATOE;** the overall mother angel talks onus eternally

**TREE;** true righteous eternal evergreen

**TRUCK;** truth really understands careful knowledge

**TRUE;** the real understanding evergreen

**TUBE;** the understanding belief everywhere

**TWO;** the winning onus

**TWO;** true wisdom overall

**UNDERSTANDING;** united nations deliver eternal right-
eous salvation to allowing new decisions in new growth
**U.S.A;** understanding saving angel
**VISION;** various intellectuals saving individuals of nations


**WALKER;** wise angel loves knowledge eternally rallying
**WALKER;** wise angels live knowing eternal realities
**WAR;** win all realities
**WELL;** win every living life
**WELL;** win every loving life
**WELL POWERS;** win every loving life poetically over wise
eternal righteous savor
**WELL POWERS;** win every loving life poetically over wise
eternal righteous salvation
**WHEEL;** wisdom has everyone eternally loving
**WHITE;** wealthy heaven intellectually teaches earthlings
**WHITE;** wealth here in the earth
**WISDOM;** wealth is slightly down over men
**WOMEN;** wisdom over man eternity now
**WOMEN;** will over men everywhere now
**WORD;** will of real diadem
**WORLD;** will of real life diadem
**WORTH;** will of realms truth here


**XYLOPHONE;** exodus youthfully loving other personality
here on new earth


**YELLOW;** yeshiva eternally loves living on wisdom
**YELLOW;** you eternally love life on wisdom

**ZECHARIAH;** Zeus eternally chooses heavens angels rallying initials all herein

**ZECHARIAH;** Zeus eventually calls humans and realms in all heavens

**ZEPHANIAH;** Zeus's eternal persons have angels newing in all heavens

**ZERO;** Zeus everywhere right overall

**ZERO;** Zeus eternally right overall